Effective Strategy Against Temper, Rage, & Wrath

Practical Wisdom to Live a Calm and Satisfying Life

Theodore H. Kittell, PhD, JD, DLitt

GlobalEdAdvance
Press

Effective Strategy Against Temper, Rage, and Wrath

Copyright © 2012 by Theodore H. Kittell

Library of Congress Control Number: 2012931573

Kittell, Theodore H., 1934–

ISBN 978-1-935434-10-8

Subject Codes and Description: 1. SEL033000 Self-Help: Anger Management; 2. PSY017000 Psychology: Interpersonal Relations; 3. EDU 045000 Education: Counseling – Crisis Management.

This book was written in collaboration with Hollis L. Green and GEAPress. All rights reserved, including the right to reproduce this book or any part thereof in any form, except for inclusion of brief quotations in a review, without the written permission of the author and GlobalEdAdvancePRESS.

Printed in Australia, Brazeil, France, Germany, Italy, Spain, UK, USA, and the Espresso Book Machine

Cover design by Barton Green

The Press does not have ownership of the contents of a book; this is the author's work and the author owns the copyright. All theory, concepts, constructs, and perspectives are those of the author and not necessarily the Press. They are presented for open and free discussion of the issues involved. All comments and feedback should be directed to the Email: [comments4author@aol.com] and the comments will be forwarded to the author for response.

Published by
GlobalEd Advance Press
www.gea-books.com

DEDICATION

I dedicate this book to those individuals
whom I have assisted in living a
calm and satisfying life.

EFFECTIVE STRATEGY AGAINST TEMPER RAGE & WRATH

CONTENTS

PROLOGUE   7

1. LIVING WITH DIFFICULT PEOPLE   13
2. DEALING WITH DESTRUCTIVE ENERGY   25
3. STRATEGIZING TO REDUCE ANGER   31
4. HANDLING HARMFUL EMOTIONS   45
5. USING DYNAMIC LISTENING   57
6. ANSWERING FUZZY THINKING   67
7. SOLVING CONFLICTS WITH MATURITY   77

EPILOGUE   83

REFERENCES   87

ABOUT THE AUTHOR   91

THEODORE H. KITTELL

PROLOGUE

WORDS SPOKEN SOFTLY

Listen to the Words

Do not get caught up in the problem, listen to the words. Individuals, who would assist those who are upset or angry, must learn to stop and observe the situation and listen to the words and tone of the conversation. It is called active listening. That means one will analyze and act appropriately based on what they see and hear. This could be called mature behavior. The wise man, Solomon, in Holy Scripture clearly stated that a "soft answer turns away wrath, but grievous and hurtful words stir up anger" (Proverbs 15:1). The concept of "soft" is tender-hearted words spoken softly from an understanding heart. And that these "soft" words turn back bottled up anger and prevent expressions of wrath. It is obvious to all that hurtful words or grievous action causes anger to be expressed not only in more hurtful words, but also clearly expressed in the countenance of the angry person.

Words from the Heart

This suggests that smooth words that come from the heart, rather than harsh words spoken with a hard face, are the better choice in any effort to win over an angry soul. Often it is the tone or the facial expression that creates the argument and perpetuates the disagreement. The effort is to make an angry person less hostile or suspicious and more inclined to act in a friendly way.

Several Forms of Anger

This book includes suggestions to deal with several forms of anger that are expressed in different ways. Temper, rage, and wrath as forms of anger can be understood and corrected through anger management training. Even the peacemaking skills of colleagues can make a positive difference. In fact, those closest to the situation can normally do more to reduce the damage of anger incidents. There may be general policies to deal with such episodes, but it is up to those present to carry out the proposed course of action.

A 24/7 Problem

According to the present society, it is bad to lose control, show rage, or demonstrate wrathful behavior. This is where a personal problem spills over into the lives of others. Yet, today we see anger expressed 24/7 on television, news, and the movies. It is assumed that this is done to reveal flaws in society. Sadly, these episodes never suggest or show solutions to open anger. A workable process of dealing with anger in children and teenagers is not suggested as a preventive measure. Yet, it is common to see the bad guys showing their anger and then be punished for their behavior. This punishment is usually drastic and normally shows no rehab support or specialized treatment for people who have expressed rage or wrathful behavior.

If one represses anger it will often explode into the loss of control and become rage. This is a no-win situation. Could this be why those who are confined or placed in psychiatric centers for medication often explode later? Was the correction too late? Could earlier intervention have prevented the problem?

No Easy Fix

There is no easy fix for bad temper. A young man in Rhea County, Tennessee was placed in a psychiatric center for treatment. After a few days of therapy, the counselor asked, "What are we going to do about *this* temper?" The young man responded, "Can't you give me a shot for that?" The response was "There is no shot for temper!" But the young man struck back, "I know there is, because they gave my dog a shot for his temper!" Would it not be wonderful, if it were as easy as a "shot" for an animal with distemper? To fix flawed behavior in the young is a noble effort. It is not easy, but it is necessary.

Learning Self-control

It is best to handle anger as it comes and assist individuals to learn self-control as well as mature behavior. We live in a harsh and unfriendly world. From the distressing moment of birth and the slap on the bottom, the world is a frightening and often shocking place. Everyday life is filled with psychological trauma and negative conditioning that colors much of what we see, hear, and say. Early negative conditioning at times creates long-term psychological effects that are expressed through relationships. There is a need for early intervention in the lives of difficult individuals. Would it not be a wonderful thing if children and young people learned self-control? You could make a difference!

Making a Difference

At times it is not the fault or the "other person;" the problem may be within you. Could it be the "sin of omission" where you failed to intervene in lives of the young around you? This book is designed to assist readers to make this determination. You can make a difference in your personal behavior and you can become a peacemaker in the arena where anger incidents occur. You can make a difference in the life of some child or young person by positive intervention when and where it is needed.   The positive future of civilized society may be determined by self-control and learning to express fears and hurts in a constructive manner. Others are counting on you!

Silence has meaning.

1

Living with Difficult People

A Can of Worms

Everyone knows there are difficult people in the world. Living among them is not easy; daily contact opens up a can of worms and creates problems. When these difficult people are relatives, coworkers, neighbors, and friends, life becomes more problematic and at times the annoyance turns into anger.

Affirmative Connecting

There are ways to make it easier to live with difficult people. It is called Affirmative Connecting. This includes elements of approval, coping, and responding to these people in a positive manner. Several approaches may be attempted; efforts to change them usually do not work. One approach is to pay no attention to them and just muddle through the day hoping that tomorrow will be better; this does not apply to harmful dealings.

Affirmative Connecting limits the difficult person's control of the situation. It helps you to deal with the behavior of the most difficult people. These falls into three types: negative, silent, and controlling people.

Negative People

The negative person is not concerned about new ideas or solving new problems. Most people will consider and evaluate new ideas, but negative people have a tendency to harm any organization of which they are apart. To hassle a negative person does not work. To do so may make things worse. They may not be deliberately pessimistic, and some may even hope they could act in a different way. Many of the negative people are afraid to risk failure with new or positive behavior. Others feel they do not have sufficient self-control to make any constructive change. Regrettably, in wanting to control their own lives, they try to control other people. This makes them even more negative and difficult.

A No-Win Situation: How do we get along with these people when they seem to spread gloominess, misery, and hindrance everywhere they go? Communicating with them is almost impossible. Even when one sees both their hurts and potential, it takes lots of spiritual force to relate to these people in a loving way. One cannot buttress or condone their behavior; it becomes a dilemma. You may think the thing to do is to take the course of least resistance and give in to the negative person. Giving in only feeds their troubles. Never get drawn into their personal difficulties. You cannot argue them out of their negative faults or stimulate them to positive action. Their defensiveness and need for control will always stimulate them to out-argue you even if their arguments are irrational. It is a no-win situation to argue with a negative person.

When negative people will not respond positively to efforts to improve communication, you need to move on. Simply ignoring their opinions will damage your relationship. You may share your reasons and thank them for listening to your ideas. You may even value their relationship, but the negative person may not believe your reasons. Moving on may be the only alternative. At this point you should limit your interaction with a negative person and suggest they try a counselor. You may believe that positive change is still possible, but the ability to change rests with the negative person. It is OK to have care and compassion, but the change must come from them or moving on is the only alternative.

Silent People

Communication is a two-way street. To walk along with a silent person will not solve the problem. People were meant to talk with one another. When people are silent, you will become frustrated.

Waiting for a response from a silent person is most frustrating. The silent person shuns you with an empty look and makes no contact with you. The thorniest silent people to deal with close family and relatives. Some silent people speak as if they were sending a telegram. They use as few words as physically possible. Silent people are all more or less around us

Silence has Meaning: There are numerous reasons why silent people do not talk. Some of them are silent to control others. Not talking is an effective way to frustrate others. Some may not talk to keep away from their fears and annoying way of thinking. Some are silent to keep away from confronting another person. When inner issues are verbalized their reality is more evident than when you safeguard yourself by remaining silent.

Silence conveys its own meaning. Many of them want to speak, but they do not know how. A helpful approach to silent people is to ask them to talk and make it easier to share their belief and way of thinking. You can show care and concern by being a good listener. Some additional things you can do to get along better with silent people: accept their silence; ask open ended questions; or deal straightforwardly with silence.

The direct advance is most effective when silent people are asked to explain how others have been making communication difficult for them. It is important to listen and not allow distrustful attitudes to surface. What they say may not be correct to you, but that is how they realize it. Ask helpful questions if they are needed. Be cautious not to say anything that would cause them to withdraw deeper into their silence.

Controller People

It appears that some people are born to control and dominate others. These people have learned to control and ride roughshod over others. They are easy to become aware of and difficult to ignore. They have a relentless need to control, and they seem to be everywhere.

Dictatorial Tendencies: Some controller people are ignorant of the scope of their dictatorial tendencies. Others are aware and have power over people and work silently behind the scenes. Some are volatile and observable, while others are unbearable. Many controller people are capable individuals, but usually do not act openly. They have learned to stay away from openness and project their attitudes onto other people. Controlling people usually provide one-sided information to explain they are right and that others are wrong. Controller people can be well-informed and at times even useful. Competent controllers feel they must win.

When the controller's projects do well they let everyone know that they take the credit. If they do not work they let everybody know it is not their fault. When other people oppose their dominating tendencies, controller people see it as a personal assault against them. In reaction they fall back on a widespread cache of weapons. One method is anger, where they are deafening and they use impatience and scorn. They also may use the silent behavior. It is difficult for a controller to live with indecision. To them control means security. They have little acceptance for inability in others. They will tell you often they are the proficient expert.

An Essential Step

An essential step for getting along with difficult people is to listen well. As you listen, recognize talent especially verbal skills. The unacceptable conduct of difficult people is similar to the following difficult people:

Antagonistic Aggressive: They try to intimidate and overpower by bombarding other people, making critical remarks, or have a fit of temper when efforts do not go the way they want them to.

Complainers: These are persons who complain persistently, but in no way do anything no matter what they are complaining about, since they feel incapable to do so or they refuse to accept the responsibility.

Silent and Indifferent: These people respond to every inquiry you may have, or every appeal for help you make, with a one syllable word like a yes, a no, or a mumble.

Super Good: They often are very friendly, witty, and sociable people. They are always rational, frank, and accommodating in your presence, but they do not produce what they say they will. They act divergent to the way they have led you to anticipate.

Negativists: When a scheme is presented they are bound to object and say it will not work or it is not doable. All too often they will shrink any confidence you might have.

Know It All Experts: These are *better*-quality people who think and want you to be sentient that they know all there is to know about all there is worth knowing. They are superior, better, patronizing, or pompous, and they will make you think you are akin to a dunce.

Indecisive: These are people who do not make decisions until the decision is made for them. They cannot let go of something until it is just right, which means not at all.

An Effective Strategy

An effective strategy to deal with difficult people is the total procedures that can correct the *balance of power* and *lessen the impact* of difficult people.

There are those who can cope prudently well with difficult people. Coping means to deal with equal conditions between a difficult person and the better angels of our nature. This is the best situation to resolve the difficulty. Once you have determined what you are going to do, the next step is to carry it out.

Execute the Plan

Decide the timetable to execute the plan; there are two criteria for appropriate timing:

First, choose a time when the difficult person is not overburdened with other troubles. When people have a lot of tension, they tend to be less flexible and more liable to act negatively in response to your suggestions.

The second criteria of correct timing is whether or not you have the time to cover the entire coping plan. You do not want to deal with the difficult person and then appear not to have the time to carry through with the needed effort to adequately deal with the problem.

Winning depends on your talent to cope and pay vigilant and methodical interest in what happens. Try to envision your encounter happening just as you hope it will. When you have begun your coping plan, it is essential to scrutinize its effects carefully and change it if it appears necessary. If your attempts at coping do not work, plainly get as much space as you can. Walk away with as much distance as achievable. Getting yourself or the difficult person out of the way may not be possible for many reasons. You may realize you will have to live with the situation.

People Respond Defensibly

People respond defensibly when they feel threatened. Each individual has selected conduct for personal protecting. The danger is not physical, because hurts are mainly emotional. The deepest wounds are internal. One sure result will be disorder of one's capability to think or plan the way forward.

When your buttons are pushed by a difficult person, you may have no option but to buy time and attempt to make future efforts to change the situation. When communication breaks down, you may have to punt.

Persuasion is an Art

Persuasion is an art in dealing with difficult people. All who encounter negative expressions of anger need to become proficient in persuasion. It is the skill or talent of influencing others to alter their point of view and urging a more positive attitude and action. Persuasion may be exactly what one needs to redirect the angry expressions of difficult people. When a simple conversation does not fix the problem, then the persuasive aspects of social influence are needed to guide or bring a negative person toward adopting a rational or positive attitude.

Aware of Intention

Persuasion may be what you need to achieve a result that you cannot do on your own. Be aware of your intention if there is a disagreement between you and the people that you would like to resolve in a definite way. Do you want to alter the way one believes or feels about something? Do you want to inspire them to do something?

The Main Medium

Argument is the main medium used in persuasion. This means a conclusion backed by sustaining statement and facts. What are the best arguments you can make to get what you want? Do you need to include arguments that will appeal to different segments of the people? What facts will you need to support your arguments? How much do you need?

No Need for Negativity

The line of reasoning known as argument is necessary in any effort to persuade another to move off dead center into more acceptable behavior. In philosophy and logic, an argument is an attempt to persuade another, by giving reasons or evidence for accepting a particular way of thinking or acting. In this context, an argument does not have to breed conflict. Provided points are expressed in a positive manner and a general discussion format is utilized to support a position, there is no need for negativity. Honest discussion is a mark of maturity.

Emotion Infuses Everything

Research in psychology, the cognitive and behavioral sciences, has recorded that emotion infuses everything we do, including thinking and decision making. The *ethos,* the attitudes and beliefs of a group may be presented in a positive way and others may see how their personal attitude or behavior does not measure up to the group standards. This is part of the persuasion that is necessary when dealing with difficult people.

Change in Behavior

When a difficult people see both the logic and the kindness with which you present the culture of the group, they are more apt to be willing to make the necessary change in behavior to remain a part of the group or organization. The final straw in such an argument is to clearly make known to the negative or difficult person that their attitude and behavior is unacceptable and there must be positive change. (Ellet, 2011)

*Feelings of anger tell you and others
that there is a problem.*

2

Dealing with Destructive Energy

Expressions of Anger

Expressions of anger in any form produces destructive energy. All forms of anger have similarities and important differences. They are triggered by incidents that upset people. These forms of expression can feel the same; the difference is in the nature and power of the manifestation. The energy expressed is a demonstration of the level of anger. All recognition of various kinds of anger provides the energy to fight, flee, or behave in a mature manner. The energy created by anger may be used in a constructive or destructive way. This energy is usually caustic, vicious, harmful, and generally detrimental to all concerned. Anger may be beneficial, but rage and expressions of wrath are always injurious.

What Happens Next

People around an angry person are aware of their state of mind and are normally able to handle the incident. When a person moves into rage, it is difficult to know what may happen next and others normally scatter. Expressions of wrath often means a "scorched earth" action. This involves destroying anything that might be useful to an enemy. Punitive destruction is done out of selfish anger to punish others.

It is important the names one gives feelings. Labels have meanings - how you think and react and what you expect to happen. Labeling leads one to think and act in a certain way. Often it blocks one from acting any other way.

Medical Markers

Medical doctors know the importance of specialized markers or labels. For example when a medical person is going to cause pain, the patient is not told it will hurt, but "this may cause some discomfort." Although the "discomfort" may produce, anxiety, distress, soreness, tenderness, irritation, but please don't call it "pain." Most individuals call all forms of anger expressions the same. This does not change the difference in the behavior and may cause one to react wrongly to advancing forms of anger; such as, rage or wrath. Providing specialized markers or psychological labels will enable individuals to see the difference in the expressions of anger and perhaps learn how to deal differently with various degrees of anger.

Learning from Children and Pets

One may learn a great deal from observing children and household pets. Their behavior is normally innocent and natural. Children and pets instinctively sleep and rest to replenish energy. They drink water and recognize friends and are aware of "negative or angry people." Children and pets both cover up or hide their mess and cry or bark when nothing is wrong; they just want attention. They express to others how they feel and normally respond to kind and softly spoken words. They both give and receive affection; in fact, often their embrace or desire to cuddle is a way to love themselves, as much as they are loving you. It is good to learn that when a kitten rubs against your leg, the cat is loving itself and when it is mistreated it is ready and willing to express displeasure.

Child-like Behavior

Scripture is clear that all who will inherit the kingdom of God must become as a little child. (Luke 18:17) The child is free from abnormal or attitudes of prejudice. Also, house pets respond to kind words and are hurt by hateful words and actions. The best way to respond to mistreatment or feelings of anger is to become as a little child or even a puppy dog: respond with kindness without preconceived attitudes of prejudice. When one responds in an abnormal or bias way, it shows a lack of maturity. Bad stuff will happen in the real world. Learn to respond simply and kindly to each and every situation. Remember, scripture tells us that "a soft answer turns away wrath."

Smile opposed to a Frown

Since behavioral science has determined that it takes less energy to smile than it does to frown, the best way to deal with destructive energy is to smile and speak softly. Remember, that facial expressions can betray even kind words. There is an saying of Emerson that may be applied here: "What your are speaks so loudly, I cannot hear what you say!" If Emerson was correct, words will not be accepted if they do not match behavior. The Prophet Isaiah wrote "their countenance doth witness against them" (Isaiah 3:9).

An Ethical Pathway

Another usable template comes from the movie Matrix, where a character says, "There is a difference between knowing the path and walking the path." This path is the ethical way to behave. This perception could be linked to a proper response to anger. It illustrates that knowing what to do is not the same as actually doing the right thing. In the Apostle James' general letter to scattered believers, it was a treatise on the ethical aspects of the Christian life. James was clear that there was a difference between the intellectual apprehension of truth and the practical application of truth in life. Deep into his discourse, James wrote "Therefore, if a man has the power to do good; and fails to do good it is sinful" (James 4:17). He clearly communicated that to know the path that is good and proper and fail to travel that course, the failure to act becomes an ethical breach that does not measure up to the high standard expected of moral and ethical individuals.

Pareto's 80/20 Rule

If one followed the principle attributed to Italian economist Vilfredo Pareto's law of distribution and applied it to anger management, it could bring understanding to the problem. Pareto's 80/20 rule would show that probably eighty (80) percent of the people may become angry and express it in some destructive manner and the other twenty (20) percent may be the crucial few that manage and control the negative flow of emotions resulting from the expressions of anger. In the area of leadership, this twenty (20) percent has been identified as the essential individuals who understand how to respond to negative situations. To adequately or properly deal with negative and destructive energy in organizations or personal relationships is to put yourself in the twenty (20) percent and become an important part of social progress.

A Win-Win Situation

Becoming a constructive manager of anger and controlling the situations created by negative expressions is a central part of anger management. Everyone should strive to be among that twenty percent. Also, those included in this minority should attempt to coach, enable, and prepare the others to deal with destructive energy in a more productive manner. This positive behavior could create a constructive environment where anger expressions would not always be detrimental. This could become a win-win situation!

3

Strategizing to Reduce Anger

An Effective Strategy

An effective strategy against a negative force would have a plan for aggressive action with the intention of making a positive difference in the outcome of the struggle. The central fact in effectiveness is a sense of readiness to act. To be effective the plan must also be efficient; that is, a minimum of loss and waste with a maximum effort to overcome any negative forces. In the case of this book, the negative forces are temper, rage, and wrath which are expressed forms of anger.

A Storehouse of Grievances

A collection of negative incidents and episodes of harmful encounters with other human beings becomes a personal storehouse of grievances that often erupts into words or actions that ignites the negative fuse of someone that creates an uncomfortable moment or a long-lasting squabble.

Temper, rage, and wrath, which are various forms of anger, have a variety of expressions. Some are familiar while others may not be as obvious. In this book many of these forms of anger will be covered. One of the most important areas of expressed anger is in personal relationships with family and friends. These forms of anger may be grouped based on an understanding of the definition. We will look at a few. First let us consider the words in the title of this book: temper, rage, and wrath.

Temper

When used in personal interaction the word "temper" is normally expressed in a negative form; such as bad temper. Literally, in relationships, temper has to do with a state of mind or emotions when one has a predisposition to act. When one has composure, their temper is under control. One who easily becomes angry or irritable is known to have a quick temper. An outburst of rage is often called a fit of temper. In a literal sense, "temper" is to add something to the mix that alters the situation. When a well mannered person with a normal temper is added to a stressful situation or someone adds negative words or actions toward that individual, the person may express a "bad temper."

There is no easy fix for bad temper. A young man in Rhea County, Tennessee was placed in a psychiatric center for treatment. After a few days of therapy, the counselor asked, "What are we going to do about *this* temper?" The young man responded, "Can't you give me a shot for that?" The response was "There is no shot for temper!" But the young man struck back, "I know there is, because they gave my dog a shot for his temper!" Would it not be wonderful, if it were as easy as a "shot" for temper?

Temper is a state of mind that can turn positive or negative depending on the circumstances. If one is pleased, the state of mind is positive; if one is annoyed or hurt the state of mind is negative. A negative state of mind is an expression of anger known as "bad temper." Some express their annoyance, irritation, or antagonism in a felling of rage which is actually pent up anger over time that boils over and is expressed in tears or violence.

Rage

When one speaks or acts in a violent manner, such explosive anger is known as rage. The intensity of rage comes out of repressed anger that is triggered by some word, event, or action. Often the individual has little control over such rage and normally does not understand what produces such intensity of negative behavior. However, one can learn to control rage as they become aware of the antecedent causes and those things that trigger their reaction. Some call this, "pushing someone's button." Forceful, destructive and vindictive anger is expressed as wrath.

Wrath

Wrath is often an expression of revenge or retaliation in an effort to settle a score based on past supposed wrong. This strong feeling of displeasure or hostility is usually provoked by some subliminal feeling within the person. Normally, those who witness wrath do not understand the cause. Again, one can learn to control wrath by understanding their storehouse of hurts or negative conditioning.

Normally, it takes a planned and deliberate effort to replace negatives with positives in the subconscious. Studying an individual's background in an effort to identify antecedent causes for exasperation can be a beginning. Providing things that bring pleasure, satisfaction, delight, happiness or contentment is an excellent way to reinforce the subconscious mind with positives.

A Strong Feeling

A strong feeling of displeasure or hostility is recognized as anger. This emotion can be provoked or inflamed by events, words or actions. Once such passion is aroused, the anger will be expressed unless a mature person can temper the hostility with kind words and understanding. Often individuals have a right to be angry; it is called righteous anger. It is easy to negatively judge such a person when the past circumstances that aggravated the individual are not completely understood. What the angry person needs is a peacemaker not a complainant.

Being a Peacemaker

To be a peacemaker, one must be subjectively peaceable. That is hard to do in the face of an angry person. Yet, it is the objective thing to do if one desires to enable another to cope with feelings of displeasure or hostility. St. Paul in Ephesians expressed the idea that one could be exasperated with certain circumstances and be provoked to justifiable and passionate expressions of anger without offending others. The biblical idea of *offend* is "to cause to stumble or cause to sin." Having expressed displeasure, even passionately Paul, instructed the person to get control of their self before "the sun goes down." Why this specificity? When darkness comes it is much harder for an angry person to control displeasure or hostility. The logical assumption here is that a person of faith should be able to bring their emotions and hostility under control. Naturally, if other positive persons are available this control becomes easier. This requires the peacemaker to see both sides of the situation and behave in a peaceful and mature manner. This is where the reconciliation work of a peacemaker can make a difference in dealing with a condition of conflict that is challenging.

An Emotional Collision

An emotional collision of interests, ideas or individuals may be identified as "conflict." Such incompatible disharmony may become an open, prolonged battle of words or blows. How does one resolve such conflict? With individuals this struggle is often unconscious but is functioning on past events based on impulses, desires, or tendencies. Conflict may escalate into a fight or contest between rivals, then both sides expect a complete victory. This is never possible in personal struggles. It is a no-win situation where both must compromise. This is not a bad word; it just means "with or together with promise" and is similar to a contract. In fact, a "peace treaty" between such becomes an agreement or contract where each side agrees to give up something to get something. Normally, a peacemaker is needed to facilitate such an agreement in a stressful situation.

Stressful Situations

The daily world is filled with stressful situations. Just being a runner in the "rat race" creates levels of stress that can demoralize the strongest among us. Any emotionally disruptive or upsetting condition that occurs in response to adverse external influences could be called stress. This condition is normally accompanied by increased heart rate, a rise in blood pressure, muscular tension, depression and irritability. Stress produces anxiety, nervous tension and stimulates the flight or fight behavior. If the decision is to fight, then the stress turns into a verbal hassle or tension that leads to rage. If the choice is flight, then the stress may cause one to become inattentive to the task at hand or they may become emotionally absent from the situation.

Although this appears to be a positive step, the aftermath can cause repressed feelings that may later erupt in rage. It is best to deal with the situation in a mature manner and never permit a hurt to fester and cause bitterness. An unattended wound can become a worse problem if the neglect continues. The mental, emotional, and physical strain can cause the situation to provoke unexpected problems in both private and professional life.

Anger is a Normal Expression

It should be understood that feelings of anger as well as other human emotions are normal. Human beings have the natural ability to express anger. It is a basic feeling that we will at some time become angry, but we should not be controlled by our anger. Anger may be expressed in a positive, neutral, or negative way. This could be called situational anger. One must look at the context in which anger is expressed to determine whether it is justified or not. If discontent is expressed in a neutral manner, it is not right or wrong. It does not matter the intensity of expressed anger; it is the basis for the anger that determines whether it is constructive or destructive. This is the basis for determining if it is right or wrong.

Anger in Holy Scripture

Understanding about the expressions of anger is easier to fathom by studying anger in Holy Scripture. All anger is not bad; it appears that some is constructive. Scripture has passages both condemning and condoning anger. A study of the Bible will reveal that many of the people described in the pages of scripture got angry. God is without sin, yet the Hebrew word for anger appears 455 times in the Old Testament and the anger of God is expressed 375 times. In the Old Testament the word *aph* denotes both justified and inappropriate anger. This word was used to describe the appropriate anger of God. In the New Testament Jesus at times showed anger. The Greek word *orge* denotes anger. It meant the natural disposition, impulse, temper or character of a person. The word *orge* was used to describe appropriate or inappropriate anger. Another Greek word, *orizo,* expressed "to be angry".

Old Testament

The Old Testament recorded that many key people became angry. An example from Exodus 32:19 was when Moses returned from Mt. Sinai after receiving the Ten Commandments and found the

Israelites worshiping idols, he became so angry that he smashed the stone tablets. Another example is how King David became angry at God when a man was killed while trying to protect the Ark. (2 Samuel 6:6-8). Some verses state we should not be angry, while other verses speak directly that there are times when individuals should have righteous angry.

New Testament

In the New Testament Jesus drove out the money changers in the Temple with a whip, shouting after them, "Is it not written, My house shall be called a house of prayer for all nations? But you have made it a robbers den" (Mark 11:15-17). Other appropriate verses view the other side of the anger. Psalms 37:8 stated emphatically "Cease from anger!" Matthew 5:22 Jesus said in the Sermon on the Mount, "If you are only angry, you are in danger of judgment." St. Paul warned "Get rid of all bitterness, rage, anger, harsh words, and slander, as well as all types of malicious behavior" (Ephesians 4:31).

Negative Expression of Emotions

One must be sensitive to feelings of irritation and resentment that could become expressed in negative emotions, but should never be compelled to act on these feelings without mature judgment. This is why everyone needs an effective strategy against expressed negative emotions. It is essential that feelings of anger be recognized, but one must examine those feelings before negative behavior is permitted. However, one must not procrastinate too long before action. The emotional weight of anger carried over time when action is repressed, can with the slightest provocation erupt in a rage of temper or wrathful behavior. Repressed anger is unhealthy; therefore, one must develop an effective strategy against temper, rage, and wrath to assure a calm and satisfying life.

Preventing Escalating Anger

A bad temper can escalate into rage, and rage can express itself in wrath. Anger can worsen rapidly unless a level head prevails. Preventing an increased expression of anger is the goal of anger management. There are a number of things that one must do to prevent the acceleration of fit of anger.

Crucial keys to preventing an expression of anger are:

- a healthy diet,
- plenty of restful sleep,
- times of relaxation,
- regular exercise.
- Reducing noise in the surroundings
- having positive life goals

It is not necessary to "walk on eggs," but speaking softly around a potentially angry person, helps them remain calm. Do not violate the space or rights of one who has a proclivity to expressions of anger. Understanding what triggers negative expressions can be a good preventive tool for a colleague or partner who is easily upset or prone to lose control.

Knowing the Expectations

Knowing the expressed and unexpressed expectations of others can prevent negative or harsh words. When you have a friend, colleague or relative who is easily upset; using every known approach to prevent negative response is worth the effort. Many hurts are not intentional and with a little maturity and effort may be preventable.

Remain Positive

Perhaps your friends, colleagues, or relatives have expectations that are unrealistic. If so, dissatisfaction and disappointment will surely come. If you are aware of unrealistic expectations, deal directly with them in a positive and constructive manner. Never belittle another for what they think or believe. Remain positive at all times. Share what you believe is unrealistic in an honest and open relationship. Just caring enough to share is at times enough to sooth the troubling beast of anger.

Enabling another Person

Enabling another person to see their weakness and limitations is usually empowering. If the expression appears to be facial anger continue full speed ahead with positive information. Normally, when a person disagrees with constructive criticism it is because they do not have enough information to understand and agree; therefore, provide more information. When a person sees sincerity and honesty in your concern for their welfare, it is easier for them to accept constructive advice.

Avoid Angry People

If possible avoid angry people and situations that could escalate into disagreements. Some people are known to be prone to angry expressions and are easily provoked. Avoid if possible. Scripture suggests "if possible live peaceable with everyone" (Romans 12:18). If you cannot avoid such an encounter, become a positive force and attempt to reconcile the situation and bring the estranged person back into a friendly relationship with yourself and others. In no case should you permit an angry person to "drag" you into a no-win situation.

Worth the Effort

Normally, an angry person has feelings of inadequacy or they feel that they do not fit into the group or the situation. Part of the reconciliation

STRATEGIZING TO REDUCE ANGER

is to assure the person that you and others care about them and want their friendship. Saying a few nice words (God permits stretching things a little in certain situations) because Jesus in the Sermon on the Mount said clearly, "Blessed are the peacemakers for they shall be called the children of God" (Matthew 5:9). It appears that Jesus gives "peacemakers" a pass here; therefore, brag a little on the person and increase their self-worth and self-image. Everyone will be better off if you succeed. Health and happiness will increase and the general environment and relationships will improve. The end may not always justify the means, but the end of the journey is worth the effort.

EFFECTIVE STRATEGY AGAINST TEMPER RAGE & WRATH

Be careful not to over react to a minor issue or not act sufficiently for a major issue.

4

Handling Harmful Emotions

Awareness

Understanding your behavior requires awareness of your feelings and emotions. This is necessary if you want to control the negative expression of your anger. It is often difficult to understand the antecedent causes of negative emotions partly because of personal denial. It is easy to be angry with yourself and not know the reason why. To illustrate such anger, the example of Elizabeth shows how angry one may get with personal circumstances. Also, how handling harmful emotions can consume a person. Understanding your anger can enable you to take steps to control it.

The Case of Elizabeth

I have such a bad temper that comes from somewhere inside and at times it erupts into rage. I have such fury, such anger, and such out of control feelings my fear is that I will carry this anger, or at least a part of it, for the rest of my life. I have all this without knowing exactly from where it comes or why it erupts.

Effective Strategy Against Temper Rage & Wrath

My life has changed and it will never be the same. I hate it more than I have ever hated anything. I am a diabetic. These are words I find difficult to say aloud or even write. The world of finger pricks, blood sugar readings and meters that go beep, beep, totally frustrates me. Measuring food, keeping charts and diaries, I think about all the food I will never eat again. No doughnuts! Surely, I can eat what I want as long as it does not exceed the total allowed daily carbohydrates. I hate reading the food labels. The small amount of food I eat is not enough to satisfy my craving. I remain frustrated.

Drawing blood twice a day and testing the blood only reminds me of my obsession with time. Giving myself insulin shots is not really painful, but it is the "idea" that it must be done that is so painful. To get the amount of blood my blood sugar machine needs, I have to stroke the site to get enough blood and then it will not stop bleeding.

What scares me the most is the unknown? What will come next? I know I cannot allow myself to be consumed with fear and anger. I can and will make this new adjustment to my life. I will do it out of necessity. I may not be happy about it and it won't be easy, but few things in life are easy.

Elizabeth has a right to be upset with her condition. The question is, can she adjust without blaming others? Often a person who is angry at personal circumstances will deny that the self-anger is their fault and they will lash out at others trying to find someone else to blame. The mature thing is to adjust and accept things that cannot be changed. This is the best way to handle harmful emotions.

Understanding Hidden Anger

Hiding feelings of anger does not help the situation. If negative feelings are hidden they will eventually erupt and someone will be hurt. Ignoring the feelings will not cause them to go away. Hidden anger is an accident waiting to happen. There will be no healing or the construction of a better life unless anger and the negative expressions that erupt are properly handled. Once negative emotions are recognized, one must find a constructive way to express the feelings or they will become destructive. Just expressing anger does not make it go away.

Unexpressed Anger

Hidden and unexpressed anger can hinder friendships and close relationships. Normally, it is best to find a constructive way to discuss your feelings with others. Getting the emotions out into the clear light of day can bring a better perspective on what causes the anger. Unexpressed negative feelings can cause illness and emotional discomfort; therefore, the better part of valor is to face the issues that produce the anger. Often relationships are improved when both parties understand what is causing the difficulty. It is essential that one deals positively with all negative emotions. Hiding anger us unhealthy.

Correct before Constructing

One must correct the elements of a substandard relationship before a better relationship can be constructed. Normally, dealing directly with issues that hinder a relationship is better than delay or denial. Sooner or later the negativity will erupt and the aftermath is worse than the pain of dealing with the problem in a mature manner.

A Negative Undertone

Hidden anger may bring silence to the situation, but the offended person will make condescending and snide remarks that will aggravate the situation. Doing nothing is never the answer. It simply creates a negative undertone that makes the situation worse. Doing nothing often creates passive aggressive behavior that is expressed in both action and words. According to Mark Twain, "Action speaks louder than words but not nearly as often." The obvious action may be forgetting, procrastination, and ignoring problems of relationship until they explode with angry words. Blaming others is a verbal expression of aggressive behavior.

Personal Anger

Nothing good can come of behavior that seeks to manipulate others indirectly rather than confronting or directly opposing the negative issues that exist. Be careful not to over react to a minor issue or not act sufficiently for a major issue. Do not act until you are certain you have full control of your emotions. The Book of Proverbs records that it is foolish to deal quickly with personal anger, "A fool gives full vent to his anger, but a wise man quietly holds it back" (Proverbs 29:11 RSV). If you feel hurt or angry, do not second guess your feelings and determine that you must act immediately. Take time to evaluate the situation and hold back your response until you clearly understand the difficulty. One needs self-control to properly handle a response to hurt feelings.

A Possible Exception

There may be an exception if the offender asks a simple question "What is bothering you?" You response could be "I am concerned about the situation, but do not know exactly what to do. When we both consider the issue carefully, we can talk about it." If both parties think maturely about the situation, a constructive outcome is more likely to happen. A simple prayer, "Lord, help me to be mature and say the right thing." An even better prayer would be "Lord, help me understand why I am angry!" Once you understand, you are ready to deal constructively with the issue.

An Act of True Friendship

Another way to confront an offender is to prudently caution the other person in Christian love. You are telling the offender that the situation hurt you and that you believe it is wrong. This must be spoken softly in Christian love, never in an angry attack. This is done with the intent of an understanding that you want to solve the problem and settle the issue. A proverb from scripture clearly speaks to the issue of confronting an offender. Open correction is better than concealed affection and wounds from a friend are better than kisses from an enemy. (Proverbs 27:5, 6) Assisting a friend to understanding how not to offend others in the future is an act of true friendship.

Learning Control

Learning to control your anger and confront an offender may be a painful lesson. You may need to find a friend to discuss your approach, but this person must be a good listener and not a gossiper. Handling feelings by expressing them is called catharsis. To discuss the issues with a person who listens is the process of expressing strong feelings that have affected you so that they do not upset you anymore. This prepares you to deal constructively with the offender. If you have no one to listen try talking to God about the problem. God is a good listener! This could be a winning conversation.

Forgive and Forget

If confrontation appears too painful or the relationship is not worth the effort, try to forgive and forget. Yes, it is true, only God can truly forgive and forget; that is, never remember the bad against you forever. Yet, the maturity of forgiving and putting the "hurt" aside will strengthen future relationships and provide a little bit of "divinity" to tiptoe into your heart and soul. Forgiving makes you a better person.

A Problem that Needs Solving

Human relations has given "anger" a bad name. Anger can be a way of surfacing an issue that needs to be resolved and a way to cause you to consider the value of a relationship. Through anger one can become aware that there is a problem hat needs to be solved. This can be a good thing for all concerned. If one does not recognize that a problem exist, the hurt will fester and eventually harm or hinder future relationships.

Healthful Expressions of Anger

Anger hiders share the belief that bad things come from anger. They feel bad at themselves and others for feeling angry. Anger hiders often think good people do not get angry. Again, anger can become a good thing when one realizes that conflict can clarify perspectives and place relationships on a solid footing. When one does not recognize the normal difficulty in human relations, they live in fear of failure and become limited in their relationships. There can be healthful expressions of anger that avoids temper tantrums, fits of rage, and wrongful and wrathful behavior toward others. Personal recognition of feelings of anger can bring productive and effective solutions to a relationship that would otherwise deteriorate.

Fight, Flight, or....

Fight, flight, or deal with it! Anger is an intense displeasure as a result of an actual or imagined threat, insult, frustration or injustice to yourself or others important to you. This can start the "fight or flight' response that releases adrenalin in the body. It raises your blood pressure, pulse, and breathing rate. The big question: will you clash, escape or properly handle the feelings of hostility? The mature thing is to deal with it!

Hostile Environment

If one evades, avoids, or flees from a hostile environment and the feelings of hostility are buried in the subconscious mind for long periods great damage may be done to the mental state of the individual. This person may have a more serious problem with anger, than the person who yells and tries to control others. Anger can cause one to feel nothing, numbness, hurt, disappointment, frustration, irritation, or even rage. Each expressing of anger varies as to whether it is visible to the person or to others. Take a look at three oversimplified forms of anger. It is difficult to categorize individuals into one of these three points. There are many expressions of anger.

Everyone must be aware of how difficult it is to understand the expressions of anger.

A person may hide hostile feelings and others are not aware of the hurt or frustration. This person knows the anger exists, but friends may not because the anger is hidden. This person may spend a lot of time trying to be nice.

Another person may be aware of negative feelings, but is not aware that anger is the basic problem. Although, this person is unaware, friends are fully aware that the person is disappointed and upset.

Negative feelings are expressed and everyone is aware that the anger exists. This person's annoyance and antagonism anger may well spill over to others as bitterness, unfriendliness, or just bad feelings toward those who are angry.

A Likert-type Scale

Levels of expressions of anger may be placed on a Likert-type scale. This is kind of a psychometric assessment of someone's ability to think about negative feelings in order to judge how appropriate their response or action is in a particular situation.

Very mature: this person has full control of personal behavior. This person constructively controls feelings and does not harm others.

Mature: this person always is aware of hostile feelings and dissipates negative feelings in a way that harms others the least.

Somewhat mature: this person is aware of aggressive feelings, and understands the antecedent cause and will attempt to deal quickly with the issue. If this person oversteps, there will normally be an apology.

Somewhat immature: this person usually is aware of disagreements, but rarely knows the cause. He never injure or may bring emotional hurt to friends. This person may demonstrate a nervous condition and have relationship problems, but does not wish to hurt others.

Immature: this person usually denies hostile feelings, and handles anger in a destructive manner. This person may have physical health symptoms and may react excessively to small irritants. This person usually has few friends and often makes others unhappy.

Very immature: this person always hides negative feelings, and is unaware that anger is a problem. Feelings of anger are handled destructively and may erupt into rage as a result of a perceived hurt. This person needs the assistance and correction of a true friend that could bring guidance toward maturity. Otherwise this person may hurt others or harm himself.

Keep a Journal

Keeping a contemporary record of incidents of expressed anger can build a case for controlling the outbursts. There are usually patterns in the expression of anger and journaling helps identify the trend. These patterns, when not recognized, will normally get worse and more destructive. Keeping a personal journal that records individuals and incidents of anger and the situations that precipitated such hostile feelings may become a corrective process. When one clearly understands the people, events, and/or circumstances that produce negative feelings, such individuals or occasions may be avoided or mature steps can be taken to handle the personal discomfort and hostile feelings.

The End is Worth the Journey

No one is an expert in analyzing others or placing individuals in a specific category. This is especially true when dealing with friends or relatives. The best one can do is to be both friendly and helpful to others regardless of their personal behavior of a predisposition to behave badly. Expressions of honest and frank friendship has a positive therapeutic effect on negative people. Try it; the end result is worth the journey!

5

Using Dynamic Listening

Levels of Listening

There are at least three levels of hearing. The level of non-hearing is when one is oblivious to the sounds around them; such as, a clock ticking. Then there is the level of hearing that record spoken words and sounds without active understanding. They may even be able to repeat the words or speak of sounds without any comprehension of the meaning. Finally, the level of dynamic listening that both hears, examines, and acts on the basis of what is heard. This level of listening requires concentration and a willingness to act appropriately.

Problem Solving

The best way to solve problems is to break them down into simple sub-problems. Major problems must be divided into a problem to find the best solution and the effort to confirm that the chosen solution is indeed the best possible resolution of the difficulty. Dynamic listening is required to understand complex problems. Such listening is vigorous and effective based on the basic understanding of "dynamic." From the Greek, δυναμικός, simply means "powerful" and may refer to the working factors of creative problem solving. Dynamic listening is active and creative and brings the intellectual power of the individual to bear on finding a workable solution to the difficulty at hand.

Problem Solving Process

Dynamic listening is vital to the problem solving process. Complex problems such as interpersonal relationships must be broken down into sub-problems to fully understand and articulate a possible solution. In problem solving there are problems to find and problems to verify what you find is valid. Dynamic listening then is a demonstration that one desires to understand the words and intent of another, especially, during a disagreement.

Real Listening

Real listening is not an easy undertaking. It takes commitment particularly when dealing with a difficult or angry person. Listening is tough enough when everything is going effortlessly; it is even more difficult when disagreements have erupted. The powerful aspects of dynamic listening may refer to the power that works to change things. Such active listening is the key to understanding and overcoming difficulties between individuals and to enable one to live a calm and satisfying life.

Open-mindedness

Not only does it take some get up and go to pay attention carefully, but it takes energy not to become self protective yourself. It takes vigor to manage your own anger and be calm. It helps if you do not jump to conclusions. Listening requires open-mindedness, acceptance, patience, charity, and tolerance. This includes accepting even things you may personally disapprove but are acceptable to the group of which you are a part.

Energetic Listening

Energetic listening is an act of caring, and it needs focus. It takes exertion to turn the focus from your own belief and emotion to those of the one to whom you are listening. It is a compliment to the other person when we pay attention. It is more than getting the intended communication, but making sure the individual is heard. You must give your complete interest to the person who is talking.

Analysis and Action

Dynamic listening requires more than understanding the words that are used in the difficult conversation; it requires both analysis and action. Analysis to breakdown and examine each word and the intent of the speaker and action or total engagement in an effort to understand and accept what is said together with a positive response.

The General Atmosphere

To be an effective listener, we often have to forfeit time, alter schedules, and get involved. Personal workloads may increase as one implements the "easier said than done" chore of active listing. Focus must be on the speaker and exactly what is being said; together, with the general atmosphere of the scene and the appearance of the angry person.

Eye Contact Required

Eye contact with the angry speaker together with a focused ear to exactly what is being said is essential to obtain a clear picture of the situation. An angry person often looks past individuals and the audience because the blinding anger prevents a focus on the present when the speech relates to the past. It is difficult to determine if the speaker is turning a blind eye to the present or is overly concentrating of some event of the past. With attempted eye contact with the speaker is an effort to demonstrate the people are listening to the complaint. Also, if successful, the eye contact may bring the speaker back into reality of the present. With eye contact the angry speaker may be jolted to face the present reality rather than speaking from the dark hold of past hurts. Listening to even the negative message of an angry person can send the message that you and others are interested in resolving the conflict.

A Silent Message

Letting someone know they have been heard is a method of reflecting back a semblance of support. Listening sends a silent message to the speaker that you care about what they are saying. When you reflect back to an angry or disturbed person, you are expressing that their message was heard. This also projects the possibility of remedial and corrective measures to fix the problem that angered the speaker.

Do Not Get Sidetracked

The best communication is in person using a simple vocabulary that is easily understood, but it is easy to get sidetracked. We need to refuse to give in to this urge and give our full concentration so the intended information is heard. Eye contact is important. When you make steady eye contact with the person with whom you are talking, the meaning is sent that you are interested and listening. When you make eye contact it should be on the same level as the person talking. If you stand up and look down on a person, you could have a harmful sense of dominance.

Listen with Intensity

To be an effective listener, one must pay attention with special intensity to what is being said. Otherwise, you will miss something that is the key to unlocking the case that contains the problem. There is a grave penalty missing this key aspect of the statement or forgetting to adequately use the key to reach the heart of the problem. The concentration must be complete.

The brain cannot evaluate the intended message if it is busy with other thoughts. When one feels urged to interrupt the speaker that is the crucial time to listen with intensity or the most difficult stage may be missed. If the key words are misunderstood or missed, the meaning of the conversation will become flawed. Once the key facts are understood, the redemptive aspects of listening and adequately responding are possible.

Understand the Process

Trouble comes in stages, and eruptions of discontent or anger are rooted in the past but somehow continues into the present and will influence the future. If one can see the expressions of anger as a stage in a process and not the end of the journey, there is hope for solution. When the process is clearly understood then remedial and reflective change can occur. Simple reflection allows one to learn from experience. Understanding may shine light on the present problem and open a cause and effect perception on the hidden hurt that creates the eruption of anger. Once a grasp of the antecedent cause or causes of the present plight, one can begin to structure the stage of recovery. Hearing the anger and listening to the hurt can open the door to a future solution. Reflection then is an assessment of where things were and where they may go next.

The Proper Response

To properly respond to a troubled person is to speak softly and demonstrate genuine concern for both the person and the problem. The responder should take small breaks and allow the other person to share thoughts or ask questions. This will clarify the path the conversation should take. Others are more liable to be amenable to alternate views once that person believes they have been heard and understood. The best way to get others to hear and comprehend your words is to demonstrate that their views are appreciated.

Some Enlightenment

Over time many have attempted to explain the simplification of complex situations. Certainly an outburst of anger is a complex situation similar to yelling "fire" in a crowded theater. Such incidents are full of complications and problems with no obvious solutions. However, a quick look at philosophy may provide some enlightenment in dealing with complicated situations. A simple rule in philosophy speaks to this issue, "One can never reach a positive conclusion beginning with a negative premise." The lesson is to remain positive in responding to a difficult person, because another philosophy lesson is appropriate here, "A positive implies a negative." To state opposing facts in a positive manner is the proper response.

A Little History

A little history of thinking could be beneficial. As far back as the 14th century a philosopher and logician, William of Ockham, postulated a philosophical razor that when faced with multiple, equally viable explanations for a given situation, the simpler one should be chosen. About the same time, Hanlon proposed the razor "Never attribute to malice that which is adequately explained by stupidity." Then Napoleon noted, "Never ascribe to malice that which is adequately explained by incompetence." Goethe, a key figure in German literature provided influential ideas; such as, ". . . misunderstanding and neglect create more confusion in this world than trickery and malice."

The wise man, Einstein, provided this guidance in his autobiography, "Everything should be made as simple as possible, but not one bit simpler." Or a more recent acronym (KISS), first coined by Kelly Johnson, an engineer at Lockheed Skunk Works, meaning "keep it simple, stupid," or a better view of KISS, "keep it short and simple." Perhaps Napoleon's use of "incompetence" is better than Hanlon's "stupidity" in considering solutions to expression of anger. Never consider an angry person as foolish or stupid. The simplest view is that the angry person feels hurt and needs a listening ear.

Reflective Listening

The practice of reflective listening during an eruption of anger is to continue the learning process that could structure solutions. Reflective practice is the capacity to replicate and expose the nature of and the cause for the present eruption. It must be a continuous learning process that produces deep and thoughtful insight that produces a clear view of the future. Clarification statements should be spoken in a positive manner. Reflection consists of clearing up questions with a view of meditation. Reflecting on the past can bring understanding to the present and change direction for the future. Such response enables the disturbed person to know that the response is not being judgmental, but that their emotions are being understood.

Effective Strategy Against Temper Rage & Wrath

When one feels urged to interrupt the speaker, that is the crucial time to listen with intensity or the most difficult stage may be missed.

6

Answering Fuzzy Thinking

Lingering Anger

There is lingering anger hiding deeply in the heart and soul of most individuals. This comes from negative conditioning during childhood, difficult interactions in school, misunderstandings on the job, and disappointments in love relationships. When anger is not resolved in a mature manner it festers and some small incident triggers an eruption.

Disagreements

A gathering of two or more human beings will ensure disagreements at some level. Each and every individual has exclusive thinking that may disagree with others. It is part of being human. Yet, Saint Paul encouraged the believers to strive to live peaceably with everyone. Yet, he used "if it be possible" knowing that humans have to work at being agreeable. Everyone desires to live a calm and satisfying life, but human relationships are difficult. This requires a strong effort to appease the anger and malice that comes from some hostile impulse or deep-seated hurt. Also, in addition to being a peacemaker, one should strive never to initiate an argument or disagreement. Scripture is clear that moral and upright folk should strive to live a calm and satisfying life. (Romans 12:18)

Anticipated Difficulties

Each and every individual should have a policy of dealing with disagreements and difference of opinion among friends, family, and co-workers. Having a policy includes working out in advance ways and means of dealing with anticipated difficulties. Without a clear policy there will be sentimental and sloppy response when the calm of peaceful relationships are fractured.

A lack of clarity and understanding in dealing with expressions of temper, rage, or wrath will bring more dysfunctional relationships. When relationships break down fuzzy thinking and immature behavior will result.

Fuzzy Thinking

Past hurts and disappointments can produce immature responses to the unclear actions of others. A lack of maturity mixed with fuzzy thinking can produce real pandemonium into any human environment. This wild uproar or unrestrained disorder must be answered by mature peacemakers skilled in settling disputes and renewing friendly relationship between those engaged in argument or altercation. This can best be done when a plan of action is worked out in advance of the disruption or disturbance. A good adage is "To insure; a calm and satisfying life, two people should not get upset at the same time."

Increase of Disagreements

Responding to the unclear actions of others can increase the possibility of disagreements. When there is a lack of clarity about the attitude or actions of others, those with residual anger may respond with uncontrolled emotions. When the line between right and wrong is blurred and someone perceives a malicious motive in the action of others, there may be a disruption of the code of conduct that produces civility.

Limited Understanding

Partial truth that produces a limited understanding of the attitude or action of another can produce fuzzy thinking. The Garden of Eden story of Adam and Eve is an example of partial truth that brought havoc for the whole human race. (Genesis 3:1-7) The serpent had an ulterior motive. Eve was told "You shall not die, but will become as God, knowing good and evil." Eve did not die physically, but there was the death of innocence. It appears that a half truth becomes a whole lie. This is what fuzzy thinking can do even to the innocent. A false assumption can place an individual on a slippery slope toward a breakdown in social conduct.

Answering Fuzzy Thinking

The old adage "It's better to be safe than sorry" may hinder a peacemaker from rushing into a dispute where even Angels fear to tread. However, trying to be safe may actually cause sorrow. The words of Saint Paul are clear: "Wherefore speak every man truth with his neighbor without falsehood: for we are members bound one to another. Have righteous anger without sin: let not the sun go down on your anger: neither give an opportunity to the devil" (Ephesians 4:25-27 DNT).

A No-Win Attitude

Choosing the safe way over an opportunity to be a problem solver is an-win attitude. Again, Paul makes clear the proper behavior: "Behave with wisdom toward non-Christians, buying up every opportunity. Always make your speech pleasing and tasteful, that you may know how to give a proper answer to every question" (Colossians 4:5-6 DNT). Also, St. James wrote: "Therefore if a man has the power to do good; and fails to do good it is sinful" (James 4:17 DNT).

Both Sides at Fault

Those who would answer fuzzy thinking with maturity must see that both sides are at fault. The expressed attitude or the misunderstood action may have had an ulterior or an unconscious motive. Also, the negative response to the behavior of another may come from some hidden or unresolved hurt from the past. Therefore, the peacemaker must use wisdom in resolving the differences. Both sides believe their behavior is fair and just.

The wise man in Proverbs discussed the matter. He believed that everyman saw his ways as right in his own eyes, but God looks at the heart or motive behind the action. (Proverbs 16:2; 21:2) As a mediator a peacemaker must attempt to understand the reason or antecedent cause of the uncharacteristic behavior on both sides. If the parties are to be brought together and the argument settled, there must be both understanding and movement on both sides. Arbitration is negotiation to produce a settlement.

Logical Steps

Human reasoning allows for approximate values rather than the simple twofold yes/no – right/wrong choice. Peacemaking is not a blame game. Remember, that individual thinking is unclear when they are tired, hungry, or emotional. There are logical steps that can be taken to neutralize the situation.

First, the peacemaker should seek some breathing space for those who have caused the commotion in the social discourse that produced resentful displeasure.

Then, separate the offending parties from the larger group for a cooling off period.

Next, the peacemaker to settle a dispute must learn more about the cause of the argument. If possible, the eruption should be seen as a normal human difference of opinion that occurs during normal human interaction.

Also, if possible, regardless of the real cause, the incident should be downgraded to a simple misunderstanding.

Then, in soft and understanding tones, the peacemaker may facilitate a polite conversation to bring reconciliation; that is, movement by both parties toward a mature judgment. Both parties must search their heart and soul for a personal understanding of their behavior and make a mature judgment about future action. Both parties should come to the simple conclusion "When they are slinging mud, they are actually losing ground themselves."

It is good to consider that everyone experiences forgetful, fuzzy moments, especially during periods of stress or anger.

Stress and Negative Conditioning

Stress and negative conditioning can impact human interaction. Steps to relieve stress and a "time out" can improve thinking skills and establish mature behavior. Hopefully, both parties will come to the conclusion that loss is not worth the aggravation and that leaving well enough alone is sufficient for the moment. As stress is relieved, civility can return. As understanding of the situation increases, there is a corresponding increase in mature behavior.

Clear-headed Thinking

Concentration is vital if one is to get to the heart of an issue that disturbs the present situation or the way things usually are. Thinking in terms of cause and effect rather that good or bad can enhance thinking and open ways of solving difficult issues. There are always degrees of right and wrong, understanding this fact is better than a more confrontational process. Often in an argument both sides are right and both sides are wrong, yet if both parties can see the degrees of difference there can be positive change in the perspective of both. If the positive and negative facts are placed side by side, the positive often outweighs the negative. When this is understood, the parties are not as far apart as they once believed. Yet, when emotion is allowed to raise its ugly head, there is disconnect from the rational part of the brain that enables one to think straight and get to the heart of the issue at hand. When clear-headed thinking occurs, the argument is over and things are seen in the clear light of day.

Intervening in a Social Disagreement

Responding to an angry person or intervening in a social disagreement should be as objective as possible, yet the best part of valor is to subjectively look into the cause or causes of the difficulty. Intervention should be soft and cautious. Remember that an injured person could lash out at you and make you part of the disagreement. Consequently, intervention should have reconciliation as the clear motive. Never take sides in an argument if you wish to be a go-between and settle the dispute. Remember that both sides of an angry discussion believe themselves to be in the right. It is up to a third-party to understand the situation and act in a positive manner. The thinking that produced the dispute was vague, unclear, and opinionated together with a little narrow-mindedness. Consequently, based on this subjective belief that is the result of emotion or a weak interpretation of facts, a peacemaker must act on the basis a sound appraisal of the situation.

Conflict is about the Past

In the procedure of sharing the tangible result of the disagreement or misunderstanding, try not to turn it into a relationship problem. Individuals have a right to differ with others as long as it is dealt with through mature behavior. Conflict is normally about the past and not about the present. Resolution of conflict is typically oriented in the direction of the future. It is essential to identify the behavior that produces conduct as unacceptable. A calm and satisfying future is the issue; it is nonproductive to deal with the past or even the "button" that triggered the episode of disagreement. If fact, most participants in arguments do not themselves understand the impulse that precipitated the eruption of anger or aggressive action.

A Cooling-off Period

It is good to ask yourself the question, "Do I have the right to get involved or arbitrate the conflict." The nature and harshness of the disagreement or argument, should inform your answer. Delaying intervention to allow a cooling off period might be wise action. This is especially true if you could become embroiled in the argument yourself. In such case, have a thick hide and just let things go until a more convenient time.

An essential step
for getting along with difficult people
is to listen well.

7

Solving Conflicts with Maturity

Mature Behavior

Mature behavior is important and relevant to a calm and satisfying life. Almost on a daily basis everyone confronts some level of disagreement with others or circumstances. A simple disagreement may erupt either in discord, dispute or even an emotional or angry encounter. Maturity is a term used to indicate how a person responds to the circumstances or environment in an appropriate manner.

Anger is Evidence

An eruption of anger is evidence that the person has not fully developed to the ability to handle the hurt in a mature manner. It doesn't mean the person is bad; it simply means they need assistance to deal with past hurts. Anger may not be fully resolved without mature judgment. This is where problem-solving skills enter the process of solving conflicts with maturity.

A Mental Process

Problem-solving is a mental process and is part of the larger problem process that includes problem shaping. This means revising a question so that the solution process can continue. Some call this part of problem solving as "framing the problem" to obtain a better perspective and this requires critical thinking or assessing whether or not the anger is based on a true or false claim.

Prejudice and Personal Bias

There is often prejudice and personal bias at work in the expression of anger. Selfish motives and self-deception may also be evident. A simplistic view of seeing issues as black and white will not work. A disciplined open-mindedness is required. There must be reason rather than emotion and no possible evidence may be ignored.

Distinct from Adulthood

Maturity is not based on age and is distinct from adulthood. Maturity is recognized in mellowness, experience, and general wisdom. Sometimes called common sense, wisdom is an understanding of people and situations expressed in perceptions, judgments and mature behavior. You may recognize these people. With a little effort you can learn to deal with them quickly and confidently.

The Know-it-alls: They are arrogant and usually have an expressed opinion on every issue. If they are wrong, they become defensive.

The Passives: These people never offer ideas or let you know where they stand.

The Dictators: They bully and intimidate and are constantly demanding and brutally critical.

The "Yes" People: They agree to any commitment, yet rarely deliver. You cannot trust them to follow through.

The "No" People: They are quick to point out why something will not work. What is worse, they are inflexible.

The Gripers: Is anything ever right with them? They prefer complaining to finding solutions.

Miscommunications

Conflicts often occur because of miscommunications. When communications are not clear a conflict can happen. Communication is not just talk and listening. It requires understanding. Reflecting back allows opportunity for explanation. When you ask questions certain they are open ended. This means to ask questions that cannot be answered with a yes or no reply. Silence gives the other person time to come to a decision whether to talk or not. Do not be anxious about silence. Silence can be a useful means of receiving more information.

Conflict vs. Maturity

Life is not a paragraph, because the definition of a paragraph is "One idea fully developed." Since life is in the process of developing there is room for growth.

Living a normal life should bring experience, wisdom, responsibility and certain reliability. Conflict is normal and inevitable, but maturity is not assured even by a long life. Learning to avoid conflict or to lessen the results of conflict is a step toward maturity, but it is a small step. Maturity is developed incrementally, one step at a time.

Experience teaches us that we cannot always have our own way. We are taught to share and to avoid conflict, because the consequences of a quarrel are negative and produce many side-effects and obstructions to a calm and satisfying life. Disputes or expressions of anger are counter-productive and cause more problems instead of assisting with the achievement of life-goals; and can even cancel many of the hopes and dreams for the future.

Epilogue

This book has dealt mostly with the peacemaker in arguments, disputes, or disagreements that expressed anger. However, there may be readers who have personal anger that expresses itself in temper, rage, or even wrathful behavior. Handling personal hurts and disappointments in a mature manner is good training for becoming an arbitrator or mediator.

Destructive energy is produced by expressions of anger in any form. All forms of anger have similarities and important differences. They are triggered by incidents that upset people. These forms of expression can feel the same; the difference is in the nature and power of the manifestation. The energy expressed is a demonstration of the level of anxiety. All recognition of various kinds of anger provides the energy to fight, flee, or behave in a mature manner.

The energy created by anger may be used in a constructive or destructive way. This energy is usually caustic, vicious, harmful, and generally detrimental to all concerned; however, expressions of anger may be beneficial, but rage and wrathful behavior are always injurious. The best result is when the two people can resolve the problem in a constructive manner.

Once you have gotten in touch with your hurt feelings you need to deal with them in a constructive manner. Only in this way can you eliminate personal symptoms both physical and psychological health. They may come from negative conditioning in childhood, misunderstandings in school, hurts in a failed love relationship, or difficulties at work. At times, even disappointments with a faith-based fellowship can produce relationship problems. Also, living a life beneath personal expectations can produce irritation and personal resentment. It has been said that most adult decisions are made unknowingly to please parents living or dead. Subconsciously, one may ask, "What would my parents want me to do?" Trying to live up to the hopes and dreams of others can create a hidden animosity that may erupt in a negative expression of anger.

Once feelings of anger are recognized and analyzed, they can become constructive energy. Personal acknowledgment of the source and understanding the root cause of the negative feelings can provide positive energy. Those who loved you did not intend to hurt or hinder you. Yet, immature misunderstandings can produce residual animosity that explodes in anger.

Dealing with what makes you angry in adult relationships can communicate mutual respect between the parties. Such expression could say, "I know you would not harm our friendship, but ... this and that...upsets me and produces feelings of hostility." Since these negative feelings influence our friendship, perhaps we could work on it together. I mention this because you and our relationship are important to me."

Feelings of anger simply tell you and others that there is a problem. The expression alone does not contain a solution to the problem. This is where the desire for a calm and satisfying life is higher in value than everything else, and personal maturity speaks to your heart and soul that the end of this journey is worth the effort. Normally, however, you will need the offending party to walk with you along the path to a hopeful future.

References

Augsburger, David, (1973). "Caring Enough to Confront", Glendale: Regal Books.

Augsburger, David, (1983). *"When Caring Is Not Enough",* Ventura, CA: Regal Books.

Bach, Dr.. George R. and Goldberg, Dr.. Herb, (1974). "Creative Aggression", New York: Avon Books.

Carson, Robert, (1969) "Interaction Concepts of Personality", Chicago: Aldine Publishing.

Cathcart, J. (1998)"The Acorn Principle", New York: St. Martin's.

Condon, John C., (1977) "Interpersonal Communication", New York: MacMillian Publishing, Co., Inc.

Crawford, Mary, and Unger, Rhoda, (1996). "Women and Gender; A Feminist Psychology", New York: McGraw-Hill.

Elgin, Suzette Haden, (1980)."The Gentle Art of Verbal Self-Defense", Englewood Cliffs, NJ.

Ellis, Albert, PhD, (1977) "How to Live With and Without Anger", New York: Readers Digest Press.

Ellet, William (2011) "The Practical Art of Persuasion", Harvard Business.

Fast, Julius, (1971). "Body Language", New York: Pocket Books.

Filley, Alan C., (1975). Interpersonal Conflict Resolution", Palo Alto, Ca: Scott, Foressman and Company.

Hocker, Joyce, and Wilmont, William W. (1985). Interpersonal Conflict", Dubuque, IA: William Brown Publishers.

Jacobs, Joan, (1976). "Feelings", Wheaton: Tyndale House.

Jandt, Fred E., (1973). "Conflict Resolution Through Communication", New York: Harper& Rowe, Publishers, Inc.

Krebs, Richard I., (1982). "Creative Conflict", Minneapolis: Augsburg Publishing House.

Kreider Robert S., and Goossen, Rachel Waltner, (1989). "When Good People Quarrel". Scottsdale, PA: Herald Press.

Levant, Ronald F., (1995). "Toward the Reconstruction of Masculinity", New York: Basic Books.

Luft, Joseph, (1969). "Of Human Interaction", Palo Alto, CA: Mayfield Publishing.

Lynch, John, and Kilmartin, Christopher, (1999). "The Pain Behind the Mask; Overcoming Masculine Depression", New York: Haworth Press.

Madow, Leo, M.D., (1972). "Anger", New York: Charles Scribner's Sons.

Mehrabian, Albert, (1971) "Silent Messages", Belmont, CA: Wadsworth Publishing Co.

Osborne, Cecil G. (1967). "The Art of Understanding Yourself:' Grand Rapids: Zondervan Books.

Phillips, Bob, (1995). "Controlling Your Emotions Before They Control You", Eugene, OR: Harvest House Publishers.

Polce-Lynch, Mary, (2002). "Boy Talk: How You Can Help Your Son Express His Emotions", Oakland, CA: New Harbinger Publications.

Rubin, Theodore Isaac, (1969). "The Angry Book", London: The MacMillan Company.

Skoglund, Elizabeth R. (1977). "To Anger with Love", New York: Harper and Row.

Viscott, David, M.D., (1976). "The Language of Feelings", New York: Arbor House.

Wainwright, Gordon R. (1985). "Body Language". London, England: Hodder Headline Plc.

Wakefield, Norman, (1981). "Listening", Waco, TX: Word Books.

Walters, Richard, (1991). "How to Say Hard Things The Easy Way", Irving, TX: Word Publishing.

About the Author

Distinguished Professor, Theodore H. Kittell, PhD, JD, DLitt, PhD, PhD taught graduate courses at Oxford Graduate School, Tennessee Wesleyan College and Bristol University. He has five earned doctorates, three master's degrees, and a bachelor degree. He also has certificates from Harvard Graduate School of Business OPM and AACC Counselor. He was honored as a Scholar in the Oxford Society of Scholars.

Dr. Kittell has been admitted to the Bar to practice law in Minnesota and California. He is an expert witness in healthcare management, has been a consultant for the Tennessee Board of Health for Nursing Homes, and was a licensed Nursing Home Administrator. He has served on various health related boards and commissions, and is affiliated with many professional associations. Throughout his business career he was active in Kiwanis or Rotary Clubs and was recognized as a Paul Harris Rotary Fellow.

Dr.. Kittell's work experience includes 27 years as a hospital executive, two decades of experience as a lawyer, and ten years experience as a consultant in healthcare, education and management. His fascinating childhood growing up with the Navajos in New Mexico has added to his rich life experiences.

Dr.. Kittell has written numerous papers in healthcare management, men's studies, assisted suicide and the right to die. Among his published books: _Christianity and Management_; _Poems No. 1_; _Philosophy and Philosophers_; _Faith-based Leadership and Management_; and this work, _Effective Strategy against Temper, Anger, and Wrath_.

~

www.ingramcontent.com/pod-product-compliance
Lightning Source LLC
LaVergne TN
LVHW011428080426
835512LV00005B/330